Sidewalk Chalk

Outdoor fun and games

by Jamie Kyle McGillian
Illustrated by Blanche L. Sims

Sterling Publishing Co., Inc.
New York

For my little lovey girls, Bailey and Devan. You inspire me to laugh, cry,
sing, dance, and play. You also make me wink and wave to the moon!
And in memory of my mom, Barbara Krolick.

Library of Congress Cataloging-in-Publication Data Available

10 9 8 7 6 5 4 3 2 1

Published by Sterling Publishing Company, Inc.
387 Park Avenue South, New York, N.Y. 10016
© 2002 by Jamie Kyle McGillian
Distributed in Canada by Sterling Publishing
c/o Canadian Manda Group, One Atlantic Avenue, Suite 105
Toronto, Ontario, Canada M6K 3E7
Distributed in Great Britain and Europe by Chris Lloyd at Orca Book
Services, Stanley House, Fleets Lane, Poole BH15 3AJ, England.
Distributed in Australia by Capricorn Link (Australia) Pty. Ltd.
P.O. Box 704, Windsor, NSW 2756 Australia
Printed in China

Sterling ISBN 0-8069-7905-4

Contents

Chalk It Up

"Pass the chalk, please!"

I love my dog

BUDDY

That's what you and all of your friends will say when you play these neat games. Write words, draw pictures, play games—using chalk. With a bucket of colored chalk at your fingertips, the sidewalk is yours! Color it with favorite sayings, designs, pictures, and game boards. Work alone or with pals. Playing chalk games is also a great way to meet new friends.

Chalk comes in light pastels and vivid neons—in glitter and swirly colors—in thick sticks or thin sticks. It's available in boxes or tubs. There's even a liquid chalk and a dry chalk that mixes with water and feels like paint, but works like chalk.

Have fun—and learn things too

Drawing with chalk helps you learn letters, which can improve your reading skills and make reading more fun. Drawing with chalk helps you write better, draw better, read better, and even talk better! That means playing with chalk is not only fun, it's good for you! That will make for lots of happy parents, even when you show up covered in colored chalk dust!

And go ahead, make a really huge mess! Nature will take care of the sidewalk, and you can just wash off the chalk from your hands and clothes.

If you find that you did some really amazing stuff with your chalk, take a picture of it so that you have it for always. Keep a scrapbook of your great chalk creations—and a notebook of your ideas for more.

History of chalk

A century ago, before everyone had notebooks and pencils in the classroom, students used chalk to write on pieces of black slate that looked like mini-chalkboards. They could practice their addition or spelling and then erase it and start again. Picture Laura Ingalls, who wrote *Little House on the Prairie,* writing with chalk on a slate in her one-room schoolhouse. That's how many of our ancestors first learned to read and write. Maybe even your great-grandparents!" Makes the book seem like it was published in 1921!

The chalk we use today is usually man-made, but did you know that chalk is actually a rock that occurs naturally? It's a type of limestone, and it's made up of the shells of extremely tiny creatures from the sea. Chalk deposits have been traced as far as the Cretaceous Period, 144 million years ago—when dinosaurs ruled the Earth!

If you approach Dover, England, from the English Channel, you can see the famous white cliffs of Dover—made of chalk—that stand out beautifully against the cold, gray sea.

Think Green

Writing with chalk helps conserve paper. Think of all the paper you'd save if you, your friends, and your family used chalk and a piece of the sidewalk (or a chalk slate) to play tic-tac-toe, to work on the words to a friend's happy birthday rap, or to write notes to each other.

You can use chalk and a piece of the ground to practice math problems, write story drafts and letters, plan menus, practice your handwriting, and so much more. And all the while, you can be happy knowing that you are saving trees!

Make Your Own

Chalk is inexpensive and available at most craft and toy stores, but you just might want to experience the joy of making your own. Here's how:

Have an adult on hand when making chalk, because things can get pretty messy.

You will need:

¾ cup of warm water

Toilet tissue tubes

1½ cups of Plaster of Paris

2-3 Tablespoons of assorted powdered tempera paints

Large plastic mixing bowl

Duct tape

Wax paper

A fork

What to do:

1. Cover one end of each toilet tissue tube with duct tape. Place a loosely rolled piece of wax paper inside the tube to create a liner. This will keep the plaster from sticking to the insides of the tube.

2. Pour the water into the bowl. Sprinkle the plaster into the water. Stir thoroughly.

3. Mix in 2-3 tablespoons of the powdered paint. The consistency should be like mashed potatoes.

4. Place tubes, sealed end down, on a flat surface. Pour in the plaster mix and tap sides of the tube with a fork to release any air bubbles.

Store the tubes in a safe place for two days. Then peel off the mold. You've done it!

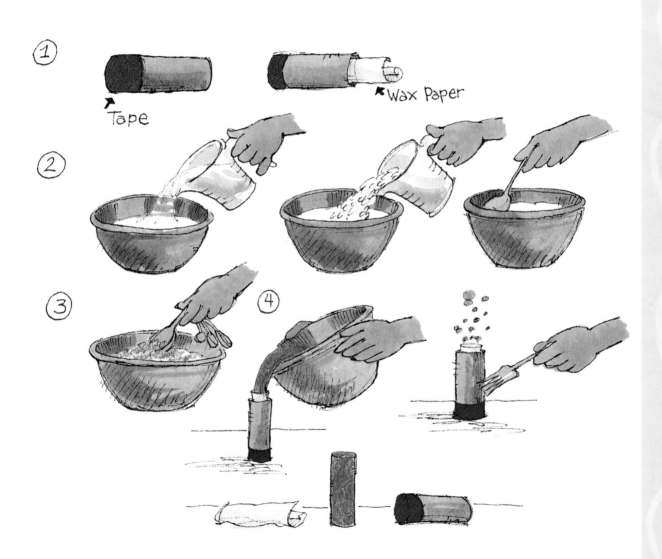

Let's Create

A ttention readers! Some of you may grow up to be artists. Now is your chance to be part of the art world and find your own style on the sidewalk. Use chalk to make exciting works of art—doodles, designs, portraits, and skyscrapers. Write words, sentences, and paragraphs. Write poetry, stories with symbols, and pictures using the letters of your name. It's great to create!

And don't forget to practice your autograph (signature), just in case you really do grow up to be a famous artist.

My cat's name is Spooky. She likes to play peek·a·boo.

My name is Rosie

Nifty Gifties

G ive your homemade chalk as gifts to friends at holiday time. Just wrap a colorful ribbon around two or three sticks. Then wrap them in colored tissue paper.

Chalk Pals

Y ou can make kooky, silly, funny, and charming chalk characters. It's really easy! Use homemade or store-bought chalk. Decorate each piece with yarn, pipe cleaners, sequins, felt shapes, and scraps of material.

Use colorful yarn to make hair. For the eyes, nose, and mouth, use sequins or felt shapes. Make cool outfits for the chalk pals using tiny scraps of fabric. Make a whole family of chalk pals. Make a mom, a dad, a sister, and a brother. To make a baby chalk pal, cut the piece of chalk in half.

Can you make a chalk pal pet? How about a dog? Attach a tail and a pair of floppy ears made from paper or yarn to the chalk. To make a leash, tie a piece of yarn around the dog's neck. Whose turn is it to walk the dog?

Store the chalk pals in decorated cardboard boxes. You and your friends can play all sorts of pretend games with these chalky guys and girls.

Decoration Day

It's you and six friends in the playground and you have a big bucket of chalk. What can you do? Give everyone a piece of chalk and a piece of the pavement. Then have each person decorate the area in whatever way he or she chooses. Some kids will write words, some will make designs, and others will make pictures. Isn't it fascinating how everyone's work is different? How would you describe the finished masterpiece?

Need inspiration to get the chalk rolling? Try any of these ideas:

Pretend you are a country and create a flag for yourself. What symbols will you use?

Make a friendship quilt. Give everyone a square, then admire the big chalk quilt you've all decorated together.

Draw your favorite meal and have everyone guess what it is. Ask them to add their own favorite food and you've got a gigantic chalky dinner party!

Doodlemania

T his is pure fun. Just grab your chalk and glide your fingers over the ground. Take a journey of ups and downs and all arounds. Think hills and valleys. Doodle to clear your mind of all yucky thoughts. Doodle while you chat with friends or before you go inside to start your homework. Start with tiny s-shaped lines. Go circular with tiny circles that loop all over the place. Then branch out with tons of tiny tree limbs.

Experience the joy of doodling while listening to music. Listen to a type of music that you don't usually listen to. How does your doodling change when you listen to classical, jazz, reggae, rap, or rock? Music and doodling go together like macaroni and cheese.

Calendar Creations

C elebrate the days by coating the sidewalk with holiday decorations, birthday messages, or symbols for special days. Use a calendar to find out what special day is on its way.

◆ If it's New Year's Day (January 1), you and your friends can write a list of resolutions. Will you break your resolutions before the chalk washes away?

◆ If it's April Fool's Day (April 1), write silly stories that couldn't possibly be true, or could they? Or trick someone with chalk! Send them on a wild treasure hunt—from chalk picture to chalk picture—only to find themselves back where they started!

◆ If it's Earth day (April), draw big, beautiful trees and write your own ideas for saving the planet.

◆ And if it's Thanksgiving (November in the United States; October in Canada), write messages and pictures about the things you are thankful for.

Here are suggestions for these special days:

◆ Ground Hog Day (February 2)

Draw a ground hog or another weather-predicting creature. What kind of weather does your creature predict? Is there going to be more winter? Then draw lots of sunny pictures on the sidewalk to cheer everyone up!

◆ Valentine's Day (February 14)

Decorate the street with red hearts of all sizes. Maybe even put a secret chalk heart in front of the house of a special friend.

◆ St. Patrick's Day (March 17)

Use green chalk to make a bunch of four-leaf clovers. Throw in a few three-leaf clovers and see if your friends can pick them out.

◆ Easter (Spring)

Draw a scene with bunnies. Put some eggs into the picture and have your friends try to find all the eggs.

◆ Mother's Day (May)

List 10 great things about a mom you know.

◆ Father's Day (June)

List 10 great things about a dad you know.

◆ Halloween (October 31)

Draw spooky pictures of pumpkins, cats, bats, and spiders. Also, write bone-chilling messages for trick-or-treaters.

◆ Christmas (December 25)

Decorate the sidewalk with snowmen, trees, candy canes, reindeer, and scenes of Santa and his elves. Or, turn the sidewalk into a giant holiday greeting card. Write messages to friends and families in your community. You and your friends can sign your names.

Birthday Bonanza

Make sidewalk chalk the theme of your next birthday party. Need a cool idea for party favors? How about party treat bags filled with homemade chalk?

   Use colored chalk to draw a map from the playground to your house on the day of your birthday party. At the party, host a sidewalk chalk contest. Who can draw the most unique party hat? When the party's over, guests can write birthday messages on your driveway.

   On your friends' birthdays, leave them happy birthday wishes on the sidewalk in front of where they live. Imagine walking home to a giant, friendly birthday wish.

Rebus Roads

Do you like to read and write rebus stories?

T hese stories combine words and pictures and challenge readers to think in pictures. What silly stories can you make up using your chalk?

CHALK TALK

I used to write funny messages with chalk on the sidewalk of my brother Sam's bus stop. He'd get a laugh when he got off the bus. Messages ranged from: We're having liver for dinner. Double portions! Or, Mom and Dad are renting out your room.   —Claire, 14

---

answers to Rebus messages on page 21:

◆ an eyeball/red heart/U = (I love you)

◆ an orange/U/ picture of happy face/2 /eyeball/me = (Aren't you happy to see me?)

◆ detail of wrist watch/my/detail of lips = (Watch my lips)

◆ detail of sneaker/-er/a/peak = Sneak a peak.

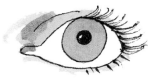  

 2 me?

 my

 —er a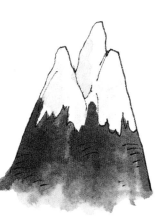

Crazed Characters

This is a great group project because everyone gets to do a share of the work. Have the first player begin by drawing a circle, square, triangle, diamond, or rectangle. Then, let the rest of the group take turns adding a feature—monster-like eyes, spaghetti arms, a potbelly, a long tail, or pointed ears. Keep taking turns until everyone agrees that the creature is done.

Creature Features

What kind of being have you created? Is it an alien from outer space? Is it a prehistoric creature? What will you name it? Can you draw a friend for it? Can you and your group come up with stories about your creature? Can you turn the stories into a cartoon strip? Set aside a block of the sidewalk for the continuing adventures of your creature.

Alphabet Art

If you like to write your name, and who doesn't, this is loads of fun. First, write your name in big, bold letters using as many different colors of chalk as you can. Then, try to draw a picture out of the letters. You can draw something concrete, like a house or a tree, or something abstract, such as a combination of swirly lines and shapes.

When you're done, can you make out the original letters? Challenge passersby to guess what name or word you started with.

Acrostic Fun

Write your name. Then use each letter of your name to make words or sentences about yourself or the way you look at life. Try it. You'll like it.

Intelligent
Artistic
Neat

Ball-playing
Rad!
Awesome
Dude

Blue and green are my colors.
A laugh goes a long way.
I love to dance.
Love is my kitty cat named Francy.
Eat your veggies!
Yellow makes me want to sing.

CHALK TALK

We draw our names and then decorate them with swirls and squiggly lines.   —Kathleen, 9

Instant Poetry

This is your chance to be published!

T ake an original poem (one that you've written and are especially proud of) and write it on the sidewalk for all to enjoy.

Or you can try "Instant Poetry":

Think of something or someone that is special to you. Then write some (try five or more) adjectives (words that describe things, such as, big, blue, smelly, or scraggly). After that, write a few (how about two?) sentences about the person, place, or thing that is special. Here are two examples:

Monster

Scary, spooky, sneaky, kooky, and slimy

Is that you, Monster, in the crease of my blankets?

Are you hiding under the bed?

Here I come, Monster.

BOO!

Gargoyle

Ugly, icky, yucky, hairy, and mean.

Creeping in the darkness like a big navy bean.

You follow me like a creepy shadow with a long hand!

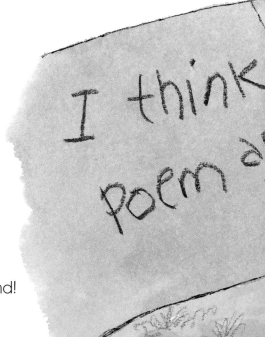

Rap Song

Try writing a rap song with your friends. Begin with:

"Hip, hop, hippity hop, me and my friends are at the top."

Add a few lines and write your rap in big letters on the sidewalk so that everyone can sing it together.

Don't fret if poetry does not pour from your veins. Take a favorite poem or verse from a famous poet and write it out on the street using your chalk. Can you make a picture to go with the poem? Don't forget to tell people who the poet is. Check out the poems of A.A. Milne, Shel Silverstein, Jack Prelutsky, or Edward Lear for more inspiration. Shel Silverstein even has a book called *Where the Sidewalk Ends*!

Portraits

A portrait is a picture of someone.

You can check out famous ones in museums or in art books. Some sidewalk chalk artists use lots of different colored chalks to make skin tones and shadows that look amazingly real.

Draw a self-portrait by copying a photo of yourself, or you can draw a portrait of a friend who can sit facing you while you draw.

This may not be easy, but practice will help you develop and improve your technique.

Body-Part Parade

Create a chain of big and little handprints or footprints. How many body parts have you drawn in your chain? How many toes or fingers does that add up to? How many people helped to create your body-part parade?

Chalk Outlines:

You and your pals can lie on the ground and draw chalk outlines of each other. Then fill in the outlines with wacky outfits—polka-dot knee socks, striped jeans, high-heel sneakers, or baggy shirts with umbrella patterns on them. How do the different body shapes vary? Who is the tallest? Who is the shortest? Can you measure each outline?

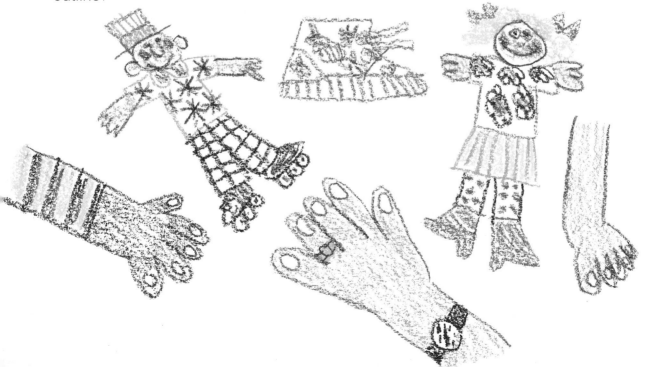

Personal Time lines

What are the big dates in your life?

T he day you were born, the day your pet came to live with you, the day you lost your first tooth, your first playdate, the day you moved away? Remember it all with a personal time line.

Here's an example:

June 3, '93
I'm born. 7 lbs. Like to sleep, eat, and cry.

June 4, '94
First step. Just one day after my first birthday.

December 26, '96
My dog and I meet for the first time. Love at first sight.

February 1, '97
Little brother is born

April '97
Took my first airplane ride

July '97
First baseball game. My team won.

March '98
First trip to Disney. Awesome.

May '99
We move away. Boo-hoo.

September '99
New kid at school.

October '99
First great
   Halloween party.

June 2000
Got a scooter.

July 2001
Went to baseball camp

My dog and I meet for the first time. Love at first sight.

Ask your friends and neighbors to add their own life events to your time line. You'll have a history of your neighborhood! Whose birth date goes back the furthest? You can learn all sorts of interesting things about the people who live on your street.

On the Town

C reate your own little town. Name it after yourself. After all, you're the founder! Draw roads, parks, and highways, traffic signs, and stop signs. Will your town have a post office, police station, firehouse, bank, school, restaurant, gas station, ice cream shop, grocery store, and train station? What makes your town such a cool place to live?

What objects can you use to make your town fun? How about drawing trees, figures, or cars?

Turn your town into a game board by rolling dice to see which player can make it to the bank or the ice cream shop first.

Take a photo of your town so that you can remember how cool it was before the rain washed it away.

Skyscraper Fun

Take a big chunk of sidewalk for your skyscrapers, buildings so tall that they look like they scrape the sky. Make them fantastic and unusual! Let them lean to one side, or have circular windows, or vines that grow on them, or elevators that run on the outside. How many windows are in your skyscraper? How many stories does it have? Just for fun, after you finish your masterpiece, talk about what goes on inside your skyscraper. Who lives or works there? Anybody famous?

Add bridges, arches, and other structures to your skyscraper scene. For ideas, find photos of the Golden Gate Bridge, the Gateway Arch, and the Seven Wonders of the World.

Bird's Eye View

Pretend you're flying high in a helicopter through a city. Make the skyline by drawing just the tops of the buildings. Is it day or night? Add a sun or a moon.

CHALK TALK

I like to draw a skyline with really cool skyscrapers all over the playground.   —Luke, 8

Let's Play

What can you do with chalk?

Meet and greet. Play with your feet. Compete. Try to find someone to beat. Take the heat. Stir excitement on the street. Discover a real treat. Play with chalk.

Shape Up

Pick a shape, any shape

- ● circles
- ▲ triangles
- ■ squares
- ◆ diamonds
- ▬ rectangles

C hallenge your friends to use only that one shape to create a picture of something fantastic. Who can use circles of all sizes to draw a tree, a house, or a monster? Who can use only diamond shapes to create a fire truck, Ferris wheel, or a beautiful bird?

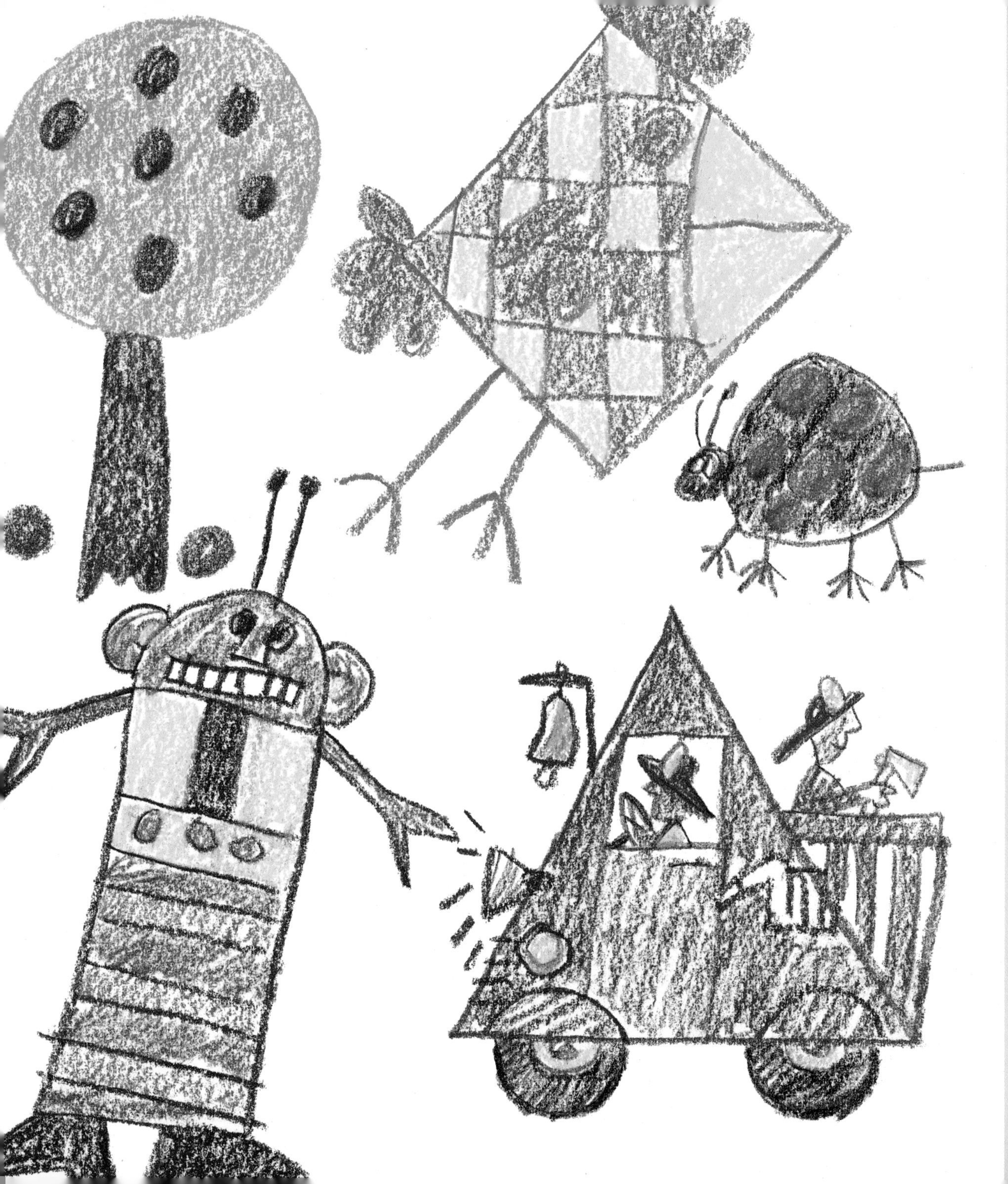

Sidewalk Safari

This game will bring out the animal in you. Think of an animal—a monkey, a lion, a tiger, or a giraffe. (Use a box of animal crackers for inspiration.)

Now use your chalk to draw only a small piece of the animal—a monkey's tail, a lion's mane, or a giraffe's leg. Then challenge your friends to identify the animal. The person who guesses correctly gets to help you draw the rest of the animal. Now, can anyone act like that animal? What sound would that animal make?

CHALK TALK

I watched a group of girls wet their colored chalk with water until it was almost clay-like. Then they smeared it on the ground. Then they stuck their hands into it and decorated the street, the tires of my car, and a picket fence. It looked really beautiful because the colors were so deep. —Jackie Johanson, 29

Animal Parts:

Start by drawing one part of an animal. Try a dinosaur's tail, an elephant's trunk, or a dog's head. Then, challenge your friends to draw crazy combinations of different animal parts to come up with a dino-dog, a hippo-phant, a monk-kitty, or an ele-mouse. Challenge passersby to guess the name of the new animal. What sounds would your newfangled animal make?

Chalk makes old games new again! Try these favorites . . .

Tic-Tac-Toe

D raw the tic-tac-toe diagram. Take turns playing X's and O's. The first player to get three X's or O's in a row—up and down, side to side, or on the diagonal wins. Play the best two out of three games to determine the neighborhood champion.

Just imagine hundreds of tic-tac-toe boards all over your street. What fun!

For a change

Instead of X's and O's, use other symbols— hearts and stars, letters and numbers.

Hangman

B egin by thinking of a favorite word, such as "awesome," "cool," or "gross." Or, think of an expression like, "It takes two to tango," or "Jump for joy." Draw a chalk dash for each letter in the word or words. Have players try to guess the word or phrase, one letter at a time. If someone guesses right, write in the letter. For each wrong guess, add a piece to the picture. First, draw the base, then the rope, head, arms, legs, and body. If an opponent guesses the word before you get to finish the picture, he or she wins.

No More Hanging

Instead of the typical Hangman picture, try drawing something else. How about a fish under water? A spider in a web? A self-portrait?

Use simple line drawings that take about 7 or 8 strokes to finish.

Hopscotch

D raw the hopscotch board. Give everyone a playing stone. On the first turn, throw your stone on space #1. Jump over that space and land with one foot on space #2 and one foot on space #3. Then hop on one foot for spaces #4 through #7. Jump with one foot on space #8 and one foot on space #9. Hop on one foot on space #10. Then turn around. Hop back and pick up your stone and jump over space #1.

Repeat for space #2 and then go to #3 and so on, until you've thrown the stone into all 10 spaces. Don't even touch the lines of the space where the stone is. If you step on a line, miss a square, or lose your balance, your turn ends.

Hopscotch is one of those games where practice makes perfect. The more you play, the better you'll be.

CHALK TALK

We draw lines with chalk and then we stand on the lines and throw Ping-Pong balls into each other's paper cups.   —Alex, 7

Hopscotch Plus

Think you're good at hopscotch? Try spinning around five times in a circle before you start hopping. Can you still hop in a straight line?

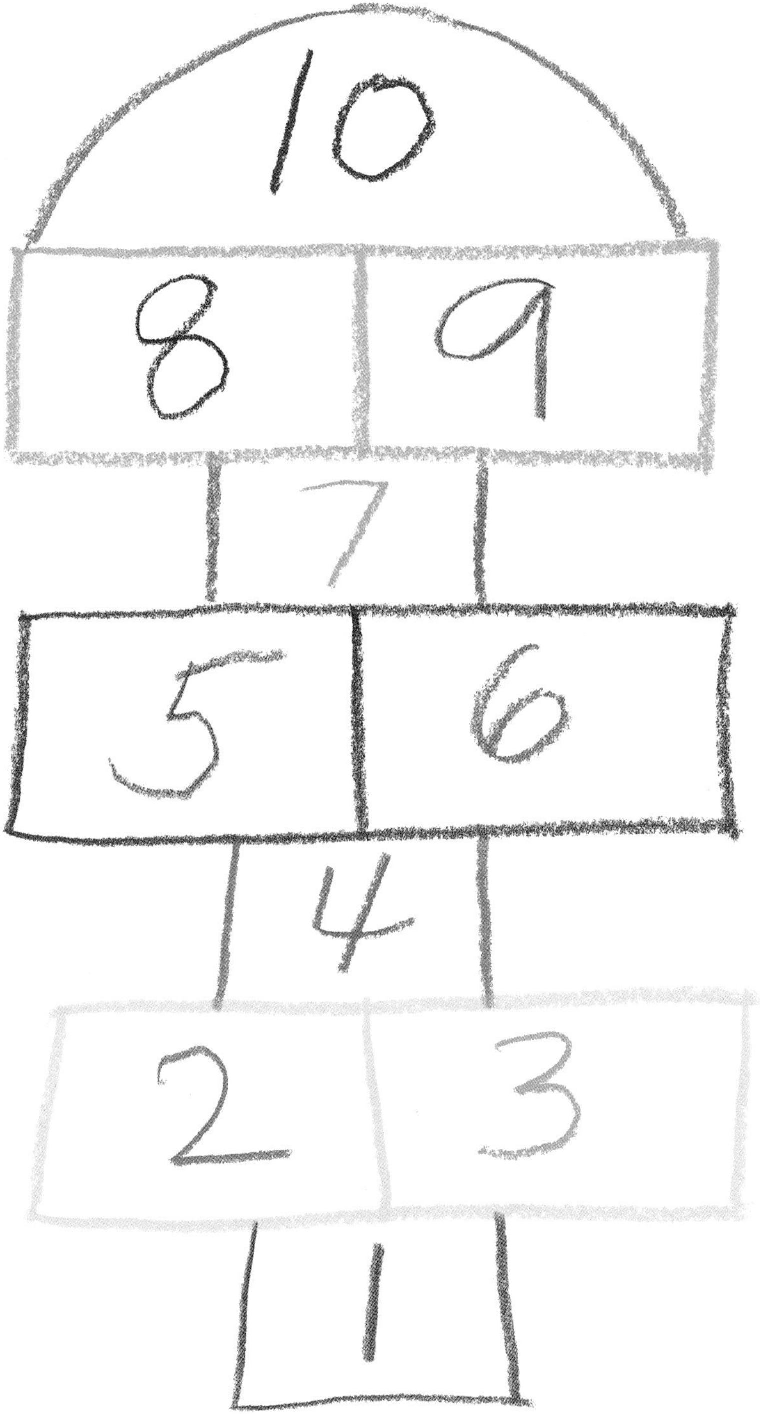
10
8
9
7
5
6
4
2
3
1

Sidewalk Bowling

The sidewalk can magically turn into an outdoor bowling alley (sort of) with a little chalk and a colorful imagination.

You will need chalk, at least six empty plastic water bottles, a large beach ball or playground ball, and a lot of open space.

Draw the lane. Include gutters on both sides. Place the six plastic bottles upright to serve as the bowling pins. Each player gets two tries to roll the ball slowly and steadily, to knock over the bottles. If your ball rides over the gutter lane, you don't get any points, even if you knock over the bottles.

You get a strike when you knock over all the pins at once and a spare when you knock over all the pins in two tries.

Keep score using chalk and a piece of the sidewalk. You get a point for each bottle you knock over in your two tries. If you get a strike, it's worth ten points, plus you get the six points for knocking over each bottle. A spare is worth five points, plus the six points you get for knocking over all the bottles. The game is over when each player has had ten turns.

Start Here

Scullzee

M ake the game board at left using your favorite colors of chalk. Give everyone a playing piece, such as a stone, bottle cap, or quarter. The idea of the game is to toss your playing piece from space to space in numerical order. If you land in the trap zone, you have to skip a turn. The player who gets to #13 first is the winner. This game is hilarious when you have four players. If you have a big crowd, play in teams.

Lots of people, kids and grown-ups, talk about this game and some of the rules vary, so agree on the rules with your friends and stick to them. Beginner players may want to make the trap zone small. Expert players can make the trap zone extra big or add additional trap zones.

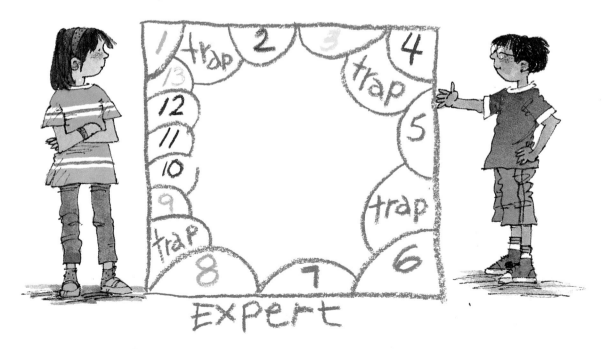

Jumbo Jumps

Don't step here

Start here

Draw a series of chalk lines as if you were drawing a long ladder. Then have players jump from line to line. You can jump on or over, or hop on or over the chalk lines. Or set it up so that if you step on one of the lines, you have to start at the beginning again. Make up your own rules as you go. Who can jump the ladder in the shortest amount of time? Who can jump the furthest?

For a fun variation, have players hop on one foot, jump while reciting the alphabet, or skip while reciting a tongue twister (Try this one: "I bought a box of biscuits, a box of mixed biscuits, and a biscuit mixer.") Who is the champion jumper?

Dots

Draw a series of dots. Start with 20 down and 20 across. Then, have players take turns drawing one line each to connect two dots. As the game proceeds, the dot board will fill up with lines. The object of the game is to use one line to complete a square. Each time you complete a square, you write your initials in it. The player with the most squares is the winner.

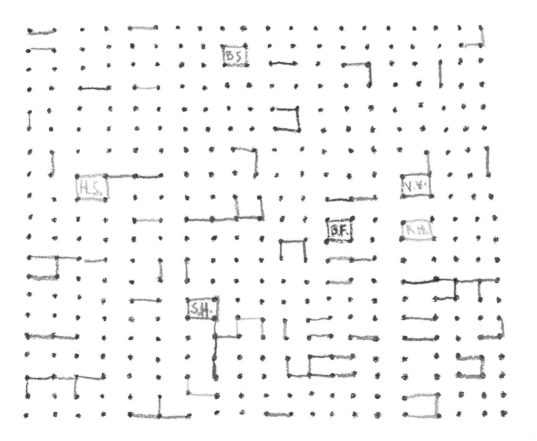

Chalk Toss

This is like the game of "Darts." Draw a large circle on the ground or on a wall. Then draw four smaller circles inside the big one. Give each circle a set of points like in the picture on the right. Then take turns tossing a pebble, an acorn, or a stone — onto the circle. Whichever section the stone falls on, that's the number of points you get. The first person to score 150 points wins.

Instead of just a circle, you can draw a huge smiley face, a monster face, or an animal face. Have players aim for the eyes, the nose, and the mouth. Set a point value for each feature.

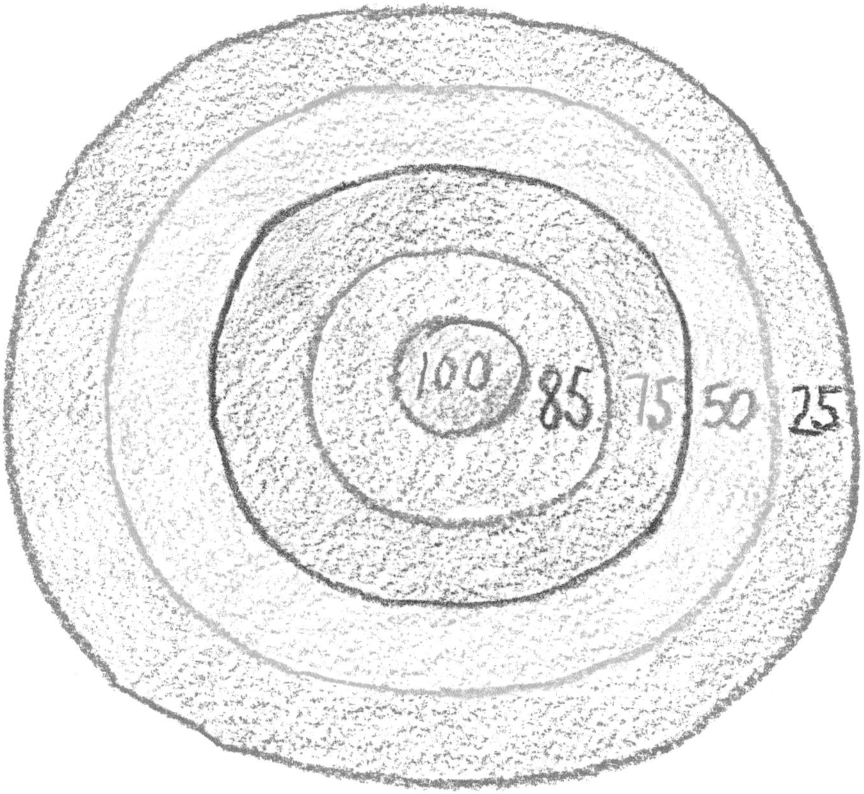
100
85
75
50
25

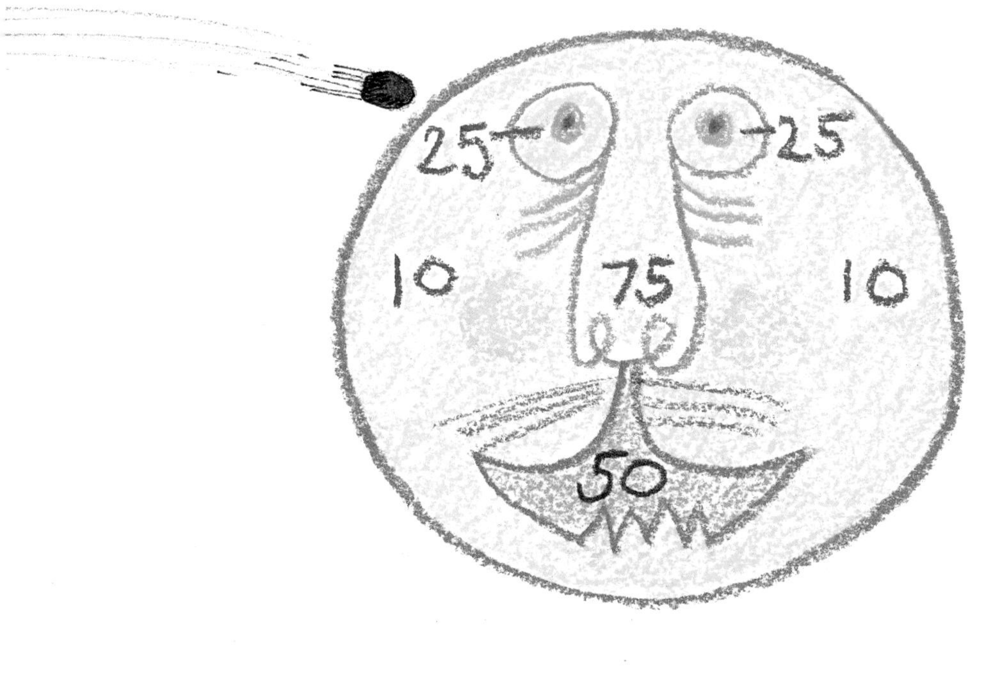
25
25
10
75
10
50

2 Square

This game is like handball or tennis without racquets. You play it with a playground ball. For the court, draw 2 large squares back to back with your chalk. Each square should be about the same size as a block (square) of sidewalk.

Standing outside your box, step into it and throw the ball so that it bounces into your own square and then into your opponent's square. You can use your hands to bounce and volley the ball back and forth. If you miss (throw the ball outside the square), your opponent gets a point. If your opponent misses (drops the ball), you get a point. The player who wins the point gets the next serve.

You and your friends can play 5-, 10-, or even 25- point games.

4 Square

Play doubles or divide the playing field into four sections and play "4 Square." Decide whether you want to play in teams or have two games going on side by side.

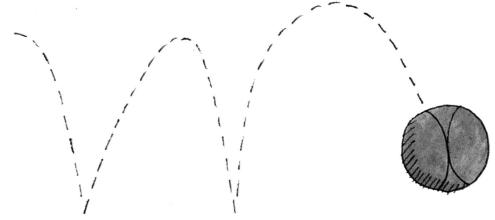

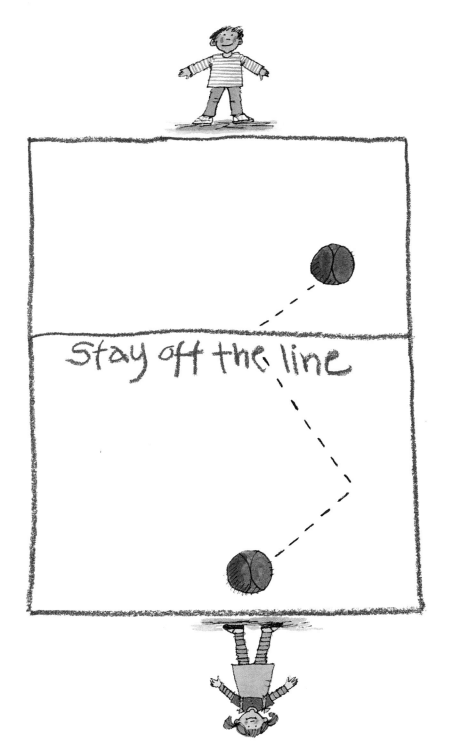

Word Jumble

Mix up the letters to your spelling words or any words you like. Challenge your friends to unscramble the words.

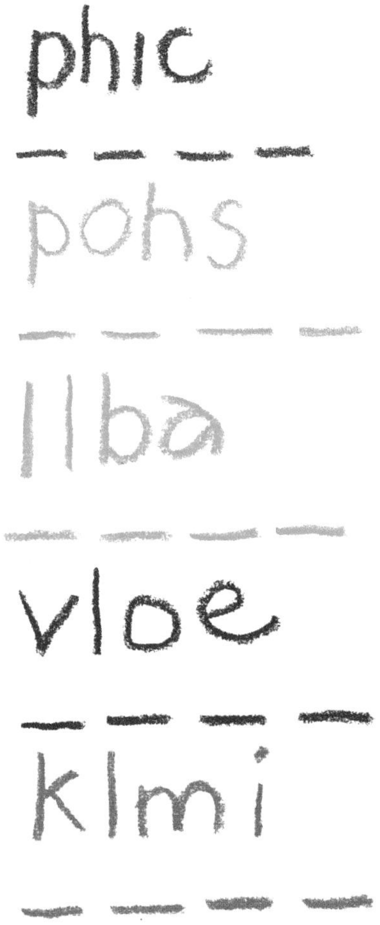
phic
pohs
llba
vloe
klmi

CHALK TALK

I like to write Roman numerals all over the street.

—Isaac, 8

answers: chip, shop, ball, love, milk

yost

_ _ _ _

tca

_ _ _

onmel

_ _ _ _ _

kyemno

_ _ _ _ _ _

CHALK TALK

We play word association. One of us says a word and then my friends use the chalk to write a word that reminds them of the other word. Then we look at the words and see who had the same word. My best friend and I always have the same words because we think alike. —Ali, 9

answers: toys, cat, lemon, monkey

Word Search

M ake a giant board of letters. Plant real words that go up, down, across, or diagonally. You can use names, words that all follow a theme, spelling words, or just ordinary everyday words. Challenge your friends to find all the hidden words. They can circle the letters with a different color chalk when they find them.

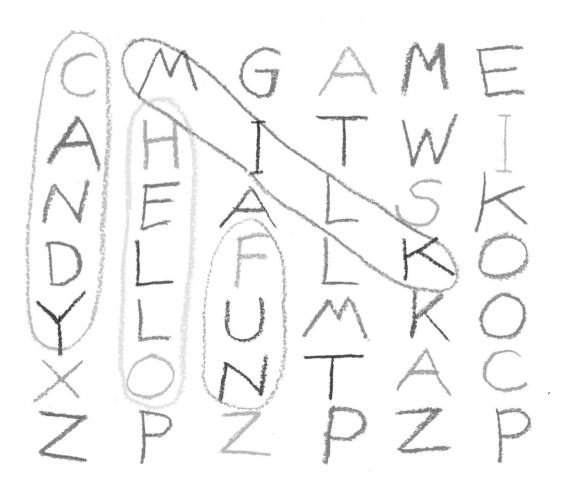

Crosswords

H ave each player draw a grid of squares. All players begin with the same word. Who can find the most words that connect and share common letters? For more inspiration, check out the crosswords in the daily paper.

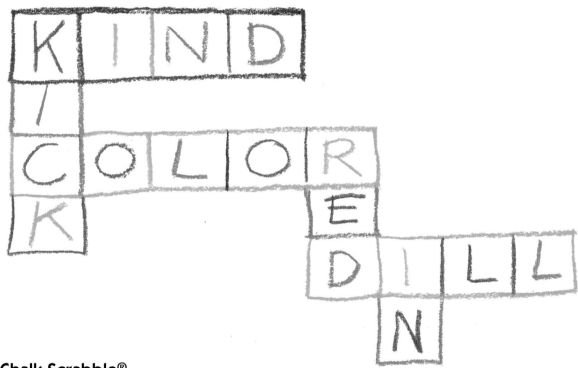

Chalk Scrabble®

Use the letters from a Scrabble game and draw a chalk Scrabble board. Have a Scrabble championship and invite your friends and family to play in teams. Losers have to bake cookies for all.

Rhyme Time

Love to rhyme? This game is a blast.

L ove to rhyme? This game is a blast. Each player gets a piece of chalk and a chunk of the sidewalk. Before the game starts, players cover their eyes while one person (who's not playing the game) writes a different 4-letter word in front of each player. The game begins when someone yells, "Rhyme time!" Players have one minute to use their chalk to write as many words as they can that rhyme with the word in front of them. When time's up, players get 10 points for every word they wrote down, and 20 points taken away for every word that doesn't rhyme, or isn't a real word. The winner is the rhymer with the most points.

CHALK TALK

My friends and I like to trace our handprints and decorate the fingers with rings and the wrists with bracelets. We also color our fingernails.

—Sadie, 4

Examples:

Clip	Bug
snip	slug
lip	clug (-20)
tip	hug
ship	tug
bip (-20)	mug
rip	shug (-20)
	wug (-20)
	snug

Betty's score	Cole's score
40 Points	20 Points

Number Line Fun

Use your chalk to draw a long line that will look like a giant ruler. Mark it off from one to 50—each number about a step apart. Stand on number one. Let your friends blindfold you with a bandana. Then have each person, one at a time, yell out commands: For example, "move up three," "move back two," "move up one." Players can tell you to move up the line or down the line for up to five numbers. Follow the commands for 10 seconds. When the time is up, try to guess what number you're standing on. Call it out, and then remove the blindfold. Did you add and subtract all the numbers quickly enough? Were you way off or right on target?

Odd and Even

Use only even numbers—or odd ones—on the line. How does that change the game? For a real challenge, start the game in the middle of the line.

CHALK TALK

We draw railroad tracks with chalk. We use two brooms as a gate crossing. Then we pretend that we are little engines that can!

—Teague, 7

Swirl
What's in your future?

Take a sneak preview with "Swirl," also known as "Fortune," or in some parts, "Mash."

A player is asked to use the chalk to write:

◆ the names of four boys or girls

◆ four colors

◆ four jobs

◆ four kinds of cars

Here are Devan's choices:

Boys or Girls	Colors	Jobs	Cars
Luke	silver	botanist	Rolls Royce
Taylor	red	firefighter	Volkswagen
Skyler	purple	dentist	Jaguar
Whitney	gold	zoologist	Jeep

Then the player takes the chalk and draws a swirl without lifting the chalk from the ground. The number of lines in the swirl determine the player's fortune.

Here's Devan's swirl:

Devan's number is 3. Here's what the future has in store for her:

She will be good friends with a boy named Skyler. Purple will be her color. She will become a dentist. She will drive a Jaguar.

You and your friends can add any of these other categories:

◆ Olympic sports (the sport you'll become very good at)

◆ hobbies (the hobby that will make you a millionaire)

◆ achievements that might make a person famous (this will be your claim to fame)

◆ animals that are found in a zoo (the animal you will have as a pet)

Circle

This is a get-to-know-you game that teaches people about themselves and each other. Here's how it goes:

Draw a large circle and tell two players to decorate it any way they wish. Don't tell them anything else about the game. Just say, "One, two, three, begin."

After the players have had a few minutes to draw with the chalk, tell them to stop.

Look at the circle. How is it decorated? Is it fully colored in?

Did the players stay inside the circle, or did they venture out beyond the lines? Did they work together to create something, or did they each do their own work? Did they draw concrete objects like flowers and faces, or did they do abstract stuff, like curvy lines?

CHALK TALK

We always decorated the streets with bright flower beds using colored chalk. I was really good at making sunflowers. I still am.   —Amy Browne, 35

Explain that:

1. If players worked together to create something, they showed good teamwork.

2. If players worked alone, it means they are independent.

3. If players stayed inside the lines of the circle, they like following rules.

4. If players went outside the lines, they don't like rules and they like to express themselves in special ways.

5. If players drew concrete objects, they are probably practical and sensible.

6. If players drew abstract designs, they are probably not so practical or orderly, but more creative.

What other explanations can you think of for why people create differently? You could learn a lot about your friends and family this way!

Let's Go

Let's go. Let's go. Let's go. Move it. Make some motion. Move through mazes. Shoot through paths. Let chalk move you.

Mazes and Paths

Mazes

Y ou can make mazes for friends to walk through, or smaller ones that fingers or toy cars can make their way through. Think of a starting point, a mid-point, and a finishing point. Add several detours. Dress up your maze with a theme. Try a holiday maze of reindeer, a forest maze, a jungle maze, or a maze filled with hamburgers and hot dogs.

When "mazing," think of the Minotaur, a monster from an ancient Greek legend. It was part-man, part-bull, and hidden away in a maze that was so tricky, it was impossible to find the way out. Draw the Minotaur in your maze.

CHALK TALK

I like to draw curly, squiggly mazes and use pieces of chalk to go from the starting point to the finish line. —Robby, 10

start
here

Paths

Make paths for your bicycle, scooter, skateboard, or rollerblades. Draw roads and highways and have races with toy cars. Make sure you're wearing a helmet as you make your way along the path that you and your friends create. What is special about the path? Has it a scenic view? Is it a colorful road decorated with funny expressions, pretty pictures, or funny faces? How long is it? Count the steps!

Bicycles

You and your friends can create bike paths that go through the playground. Make 2 lanes. Double solid lines mean no passing. Dotted lines mean if the coast is clear, it's all right to pass. Who is the best bike rider?

Obstacle courses

Make a treacherous obstacle course with an extra narrow road and a lot of sharp turns. Place obstacles on the road. Compete for the best time. Obstacle courses can help you build teamwork skills, increase strength, and have a blow-out good time. Use the chalk to draw unexpected obstacles— a river, an army of snakes, a tiger.

Watch out for the shark!

walk/skate around the chalk bucket

Beware of the snakes!

Don't step into the holes

If you touch the cave start over

FINISH you're cool

Grab a piece of chalk

Helmet, walk/skate/ bike around it. If you touch it, start over.

Don't knock over the soda cans

Watch the scooter

Start here

Watch it. Very narrow here

Rollerblades

S kate along a colorful chalk path that makes a large circle or oval. Make your path nice and wide so that skaters can skate together three or four across. Riding the path over and over will help you practice your technique.

Walk the Line

Use your chalk to draw a curvy line. The idea is to walk the line without stepping off it. If you do step off, you'll have to start at the beginning again. Who can stay on track? Who can walk the line in the shortest time?

   For added fun, designate places in the line where players must hop, skip, or jump.

CHALK TALK

I like to make a colorful path of designs up to my door. Dad calls it the red carpet.
—Matthew, 12

Scooters

Have you got a scooter? You and your friends can make colorful scooter paths with chalk. Make sure to make two paths, one coming, one going. Along the scooter path, create some cool hangouts with your chalk. Draw an ice cream shop, a park, a swimming pool, or a tree house.

Scooter Doodle

Take a load off, sit on your scooter, and doodle to your heart's content. As you doodle, go back and forth on your scooter. Use your scooter as a belly rest as you decorate the sidewalk face down.

Scooter Parking

You and your friends can create funky parking spaces for your scooter. Write your name in your spot and decorate it to your heart's content. Whose scooter spot is most like him or her? This is also fun for a party if you invite your guests to scooter or bicycle or rollerblade over. Won't they be surprised at finding their very own parking space in your driveway!

Secret Hideout

You and a few friends can establish a secret hideout. Draw a chalk map that leads to the hideout. Challenge scooter riders to decipher the map, and ride to the hideout. First one to find it gets a high five.

Follow the Trail

It's Mission Impossible, but you've got your chalk.

Y our assignment is to leave a trail of clues for your partner so he or she will be able to find the treasure—or you—or both. Write clues and symbols to let your partner know where danger lurks, where the treasure is, and where you are hiding.

Use any of these chalk clues and symbols:

- ◆ arrows = this way
- ◆ stop signs = stop
- ◆ footsteps = someone was here
- ◆ happy faces = good news
- ◆ mittens = you're getting warmer
- ◆ popsicle = you're getting colder

You can make up all sorts of symbols with your friends. Take turns making and following a trail.

Add a riddle to the trail. If you guess the riddle, you can keep going.

What has 2 arms and no legs, but still runs? (a clock) For example:

Hobos were homeless people who rode the rails during the Great Depression

(1929-1939). These drifters wandered in search of free food and shelter. They often left messages using words, pictures, and symbols to give their fellow hobos a heads up to food, shelter, and danger. What secret messages could you leave your friends?

Clues:

Make tricky clues for detectives on scooters, such as: Go left at the basketball court, glide on your scooter for 1 minute, then look on the ground for the next clue.

Index